london in the thirties

london in the thirties
bill brandt

INTRODUCTION BY MARK HAWORTH-BOOTH

PANTHEON BOOKS
NEW YORK

Library of Congress Cataloging in Publication Data

Brandt, Bill.
    London in the thirties.

    1. London (England)—Social life and customs—20th century—
Pictorial works.   2. London (England)—Social conditions—
20th century—Pictorial works.
I. Title.   II. Title: London in the 30s.
DA684.B7379   1984   942.1'083   83-43161
ISBN 0-394-53565-0

Publisher's Note: Bill Brandt personally supervised the reproduction of
the prints in this book, and gave his full approval to the final appearance
of the collection.

Manufactured in Great Britain

First American Edition

Designed by Naomi Osnos

CONTENTS

INTRODUCTION

The death of Bill Brandt on December 20, 1983, marked the end of an era. Born in 1904, Bill Brandt became Britain's most outstanding twentieth-century photographer. He excelled at every level and on every front—from his incisive social documentation during the 1930s and his reporting of the Blackout and Blitz of World War II, to his pantheon of international portraits and his profound exploration of the nude.

London in the Thirties is the last collection of Brandt's work produced in his lifetime. The photographs he chose for the book reflect his deep and perceptive involvement in the life of the city in which he found his roots, made his friendships, and built his career. London's subtlety and variety answered the needs of his complex sensibility. He pursued the nuances of its life during the thirties with the ardor of a young poet. He was in love with London, and he provided an extraordinary visual document of the city.

In later life, it was Bill Brandt's foible to say that he was born, like his father, in South London, although he was, in fact, born in Hamburg, Germany. His head already full of tales of London and its splendors, he settled in the city in 1931.*

In 1928, Ezra Pound, a family friend, provided an introduction to Man Ray in Paris, and thus Brandt was able to work with one of the greatest talents of the time and to witness the heyday of Surrealist Paris. Brandt later recalled that Man Ray, simultaneously immersed in Surrealist experiments and a flourishing society career as a portraitist, "had a new way of looking at the world. He saw everything differently. This gave me a new excitement about photography and about the world as well." Man Ray was no respecter of traditions in the arts, and throughout his life Brandt was amused and obstinate in the face of prevailing dogma. "Photography is still a very new medium," he once wrote, "and everything must be tried and dared. . . . Photography has no *rules*. It is not a *sport*. It is the result which counts, no matter how it was achieved."

Brandt was one of a generation of young photographic explorers whose visas, it could be said, had already been issued by literature. Knut Hamsun's

novel *Hunger,* published in 1890, displayed a photographic sensibility. Hamsun's young hero seizes, or is seized by, split-second images in the street. The tiniest scraps of movement, like a woman opening an upstairs window, pass through the lens of his eyes and are imprinted on the retina. In *Le Paysan de Paris,* published in 1926 (translated by Simon Watson as *Paris Peasant* in 1971), Louis Aragon made explicit the connections between writing, Surrealism, photography, and the pace and intricacy of the modern city. "Let us enter the Baths of the Passage de l'Opéra with a practical mind. And a little Kodak." Aragon announced to the world "this momentous news item: a new vice has just been born; man has acquired one more source of vertigo—Surrealism, offspring of frenzy and darkness. Walk up, walk up, this is the entrance to the realms of the instantaneous, the world of snapshot."

During the time Brandt worked with Man Ray, new technical possibilities were opening up for those photographers who could see them. The Rolleiflex, a great professional camera, was introduced in 1929. Its twin-lens reflex allowed photographers to compose the world with a new ease, clarity, and rigor, and the camera itself was relatively discreet. In 1930, the flash bulb arrived on the market. With the combustion enclosed in glass, it was domesticated and unalarming compared to earlier technology. These two new tools completed Brandt's essential equipment and allowed him to explore new, nocturnal territories.

In Germany, other technological developments created a new marketplace for photography. The high-speed printing presses that emerged in the late twenties, together with innovations in magazine layout from Munich and Berlin, made possible the production of the new illustrated magazines that appeared across Europe. Brandt was among those who provided picture stories for *Weekly Illustrated* (founded in 1934), *Lilliput* (founded in 1937), and *Picture Post* (founded in 1938). (Sir Tom Hopkinson, editor of *Picture Post,* recalls that Brandt always cropped his pictures to the essentials, leaving nothing to spare for the layout editor, who had to fit the pages of the magazine.)

Photojournalists were and are quintessentially modern figures—ubiquitous, privileged, and

---

*I have told the story of Brandt's early years in the Victoria and Albert Museum catalog *Bill Brandt's Literary Britain,* 1984.

somewhat guileful. Assignments from the magazines provided Brandt with access to the Royal Enclosure at Ascot—and to the cells at Wormwood Scrubs Prison. His Mayfair and Kensington drawing rooms, with backgammon after dinner, are observed with the impunity of an ornithologist in a hide.

Though his tools and outlook were quintessentially modern, Brandt's photographs echo the Victorian imagery of the city. In May 1939, *Lilliput* published *Unchanging London,* a set of wood engravings from Gustave Doré's *London* (1872), with modern pictures of the same subjects by Brandt. A plate of Doré's "Hayboats on the Thames" was juxtaposed with Brandt's "Early Morning on the River" (plate 38); Doré's "They read the Bible in night refuges then" was opposite a Brandt photograph captioned "They still have to sleep in doss-houses" (plate 35); and Doré's "The Bull's Eye" (police constables throwing torchlight on loungers in an alley) was paired with "The Corner Beat" (plate 32). Brandt staged this photograph without the policeman who unexpectedly turned the corner and, to Brandt's pleased astonishment, stood perfectly still while Brandt made an exposure.

When the photographs in *London in the Thirties* were first published, fifty years ago, they were printed in the low-key manner of the day—compare the early prints of Cartier-Bresson, Kertesz, or Ansel Adams. In the fifties, Brandt radically changed his printing style, printing on hard, high-contrast papers, solidifying his blacks and opening out his whites to form dazzling chiaroscuro patterns. He was particularly impressed by the harsh printing in William Klein's photographs of the fifties, and they may have inspired Brandt to change his own printing style.

Throughout his career, Brandt used photographs to tell stories, and *London in the Thirties* is a collection of three stories. Each opens with a view of one of the bridges over the Thames in the early morning and progresses more or less chronologically through the course of a day. In the first section Brandt tells the story of the London poor, notably those of the East End. He presents intimate pictures of bedrooms in Bethnal Green, alleys and wharves in dockland, the genial life of the pub, and the fringes of the underworld in Soho. In the second section, he shows middle-class life—a butcher in Notting Hill Gate, a cricket match in Regent's Park. The third section moves into the *beau monde* of Kensington, Mayfair, and Park Lane, and the dramatis personae include the young Kenneth Clark, director of the National Gallery, taking tea with his wife beneath a late Cézanne, *Le Château Noir* (plate 79).

For Brandt, the power of a collection of photographs depended on its variety. His picture of society is held in firm focus. Scenes are calibrated by class differences. Extremes do not quite meet, except at the racetrack, but they are bridged in multifarious ways. His sensitive eye conveys both the social intensity of couples at what one suspects may be crucial moments and the unconscious absorption of old and young in the last rites of the day: brushing teeth or reading by the light of the bedside lamp. When exploring the London of the rich, he presents it first as if from "downstairs." We see a style of life in which one set of people tends to the needs of another. Nigel Henderson, who photographed London's East End in the late forties and is best known as a founder of the New Brutalism and Pop Art, said of Brandt's work:

He senses this portentous view of the Baldwinian era—wooden faces, iron closures—the uncompromising severity of the social caste system. In his marvelous photograph [plate 86], the two house-parlour maids, prepared to wait at table, have eyes loaded like blunderbusses. Their starched caps and cuffs, their poker backs, mirror the terrible rectitude of learned attitudes. They have that same irritated loathing in defence of caste that shows in portraits of Evelyn Waugh.

Of the same photograph, Walker Evans wrote: "This picture is Brandt striking home (in all senses of the word). Instantaneous precision is only the beginning of its quality; it proceeds to a lot more: surgical detachment, wit, theater."

—Mark Haworth-Booth
Victoria and Albert Museum
London

1

4

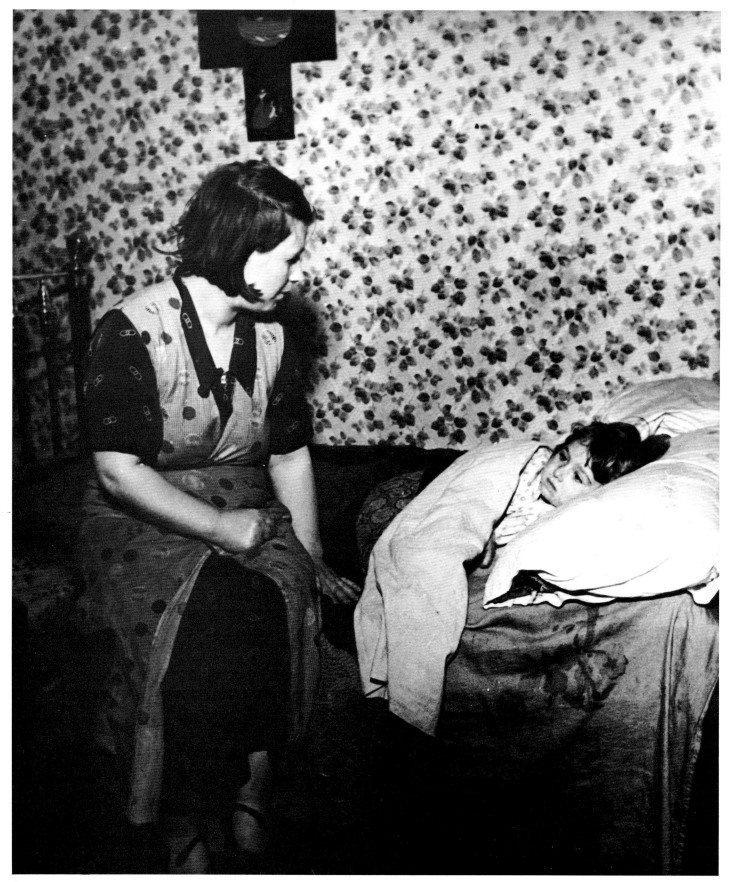

7

23

34

40

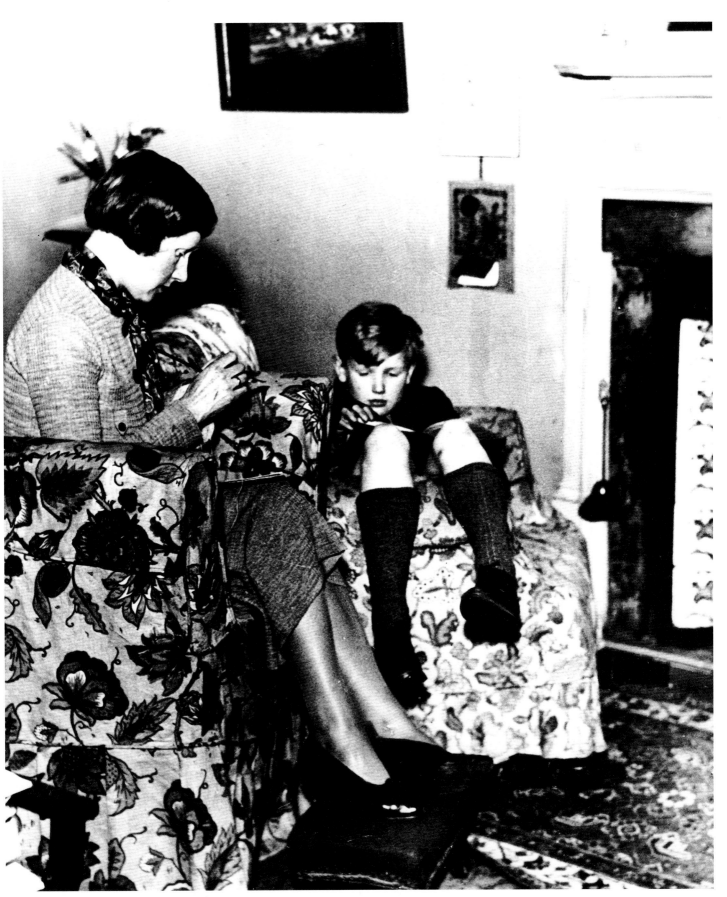

49

HENDON CHURCH END

FINCHLEY ROAD
OXFORD STREET
REGENT STREET
PICCADILLY CIRCUS
CHARING CROSS
CANNON STREET

3

DUNLOP

FIT

CANNED
FILTRATE
OIL

DAILY
HERALD
£2,500
FOR
STAR
GAZING

56

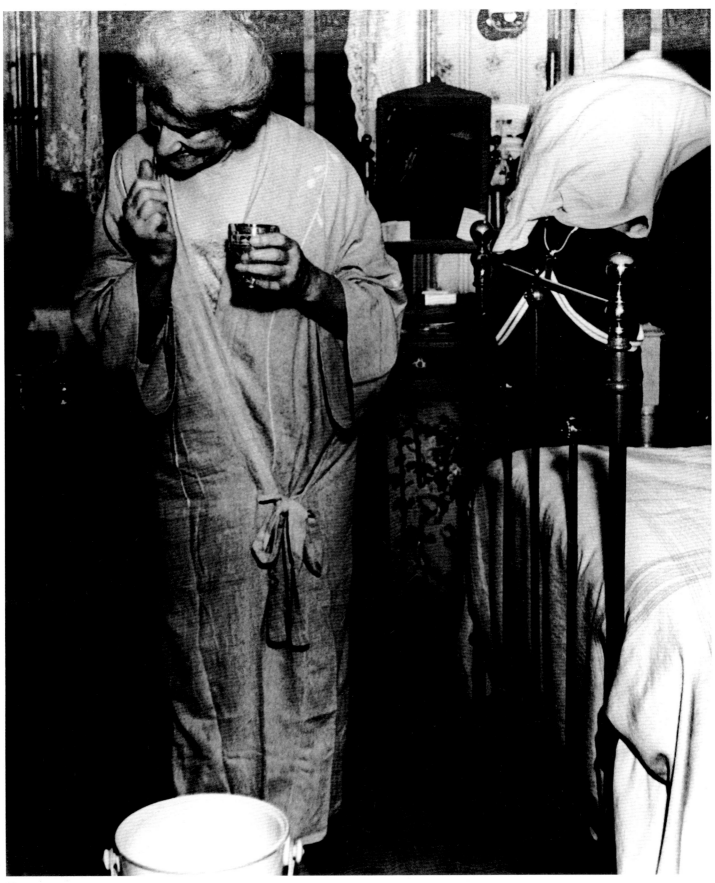

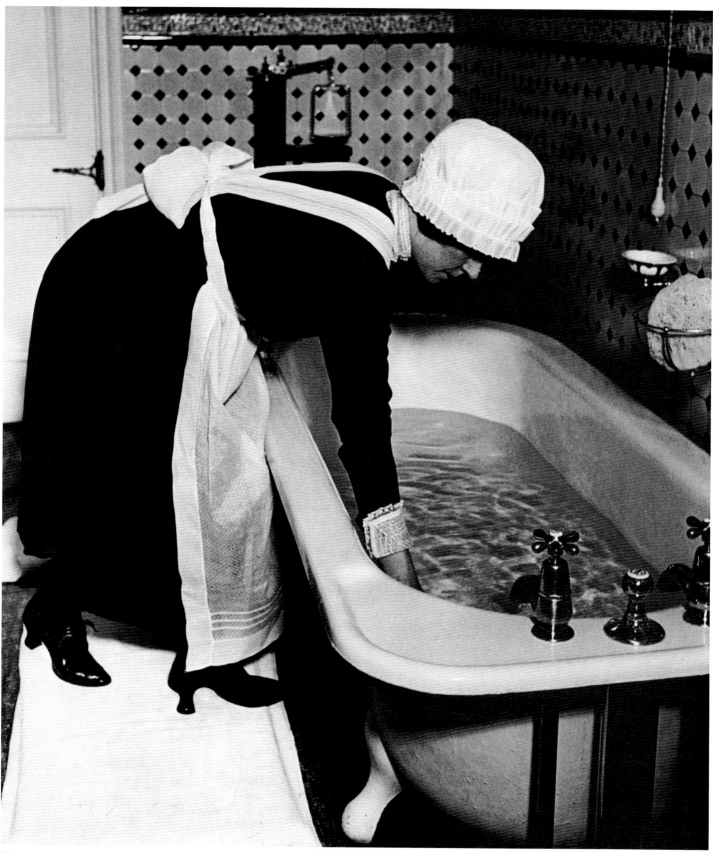

93

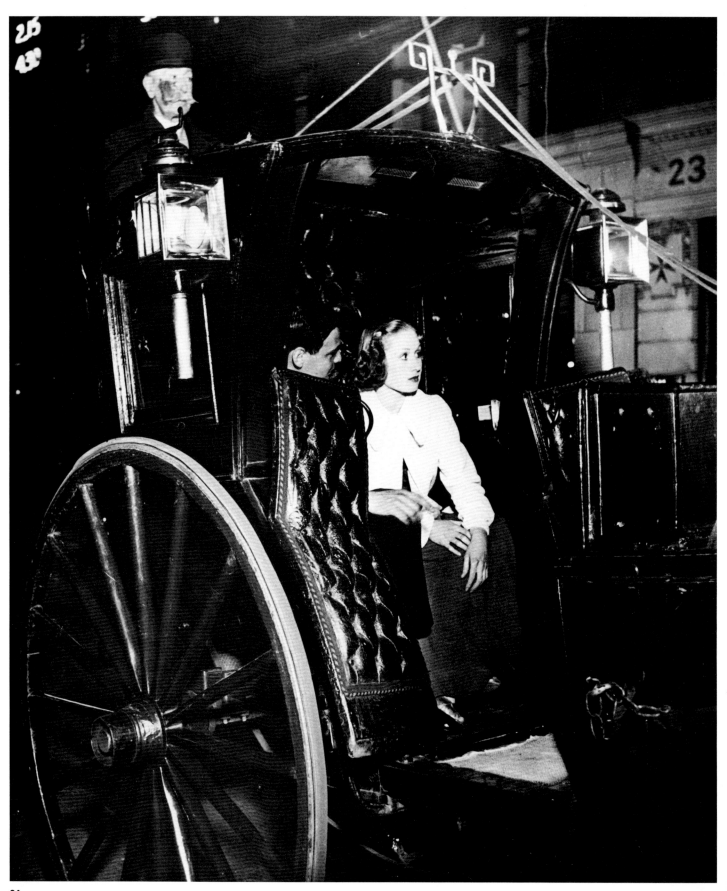